BALLPARK

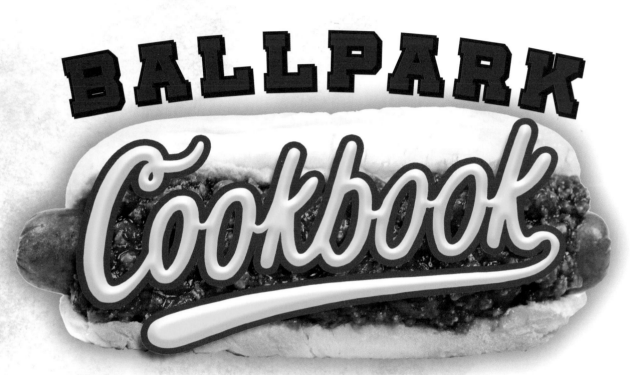

THE AMERICAN LEAGUE

RECIPES INSPIRED BY
Baseball Stadium Foods

★ BY ★

Katrina Jorgensen

CAPSTONE PRESS
a Capstone imprint

Table of Contents

East Division

Central Division

West Division

BAL

ORIOLE PARK
AT CAMDEN YARDS

LOCATION
Baltimore, Maryland
OPENED
1992
CAPACITY
45,971
NICKNAMES
The Yard
Birdland
The House That Cal Built

Oriole Park at Camden Yards is home to the Baltimore Orioles. Opening on April 6, 1992, the stadium became the first of the so-called "retro" ballparks. In contrast to large, multipurpose stadiums, such as the Orioles's former Memorial Stadium, the throwback features of Camden Yards reminded fans of ballparks of yesteryear: downtown location, limited capacity, and amazing views. Fans at Camden Yards have witnessed many great moments in baseball history, but perhaps none greater than Cal Ripken Jr.'s record-setting 2,131st consecutive game on September 6, 1995. In fact, the ballpark itself is sometimes referred to as "The House that Cal Built."

MARYLAND CRAB CAKE SLIDERS

with TARTAR SAUCE & BERRY SPRITZER

Located in downtown Baltimore, Maryland, Camden Yards sits only miles away from the salty waters of Chesapeake Bay. For generations, the bay has inspired and supported the local cuisine, including Baltimore's favorite treat: crab cakes. These crisp, buttery patties of crabmeat are a perfect seventh-inning snack for any baseball fan.

MARYLAND CRAB CAKE SLIDERS

PREP	COOK	MAKES
15 MINUTES	10 MINUTES	8 SLIDERS

INGREDIENTS

◇	1/4 bunch	flat-leaf parsley
◇	4	green onions
◇	12 ounces	lump crabmeat, drained
◇	1/2 cup	mayonnaise
◇	2	eggs
◇	1 cup	panko bread crumbs
◇	1 teaspoon	seafood seasoning
◇	1/4 teaspoon	salt
◇	1/2 teaspoon	ground black pepper
◇	2 tablespoons	oil, for frying
◇	8	slider buns
◇	8 leaves	lettuce

1. Chop parsley and green onion finely and place in a mixing bowl.

2. Add crabmeat, mayonnaise, eggs, bread crumbs, seafood seasoning, salt, and black pepper. Mix lightly with a fork until combined.

3. Separate the crab cake mix into 8 equal pieces. Shape into patties.

4. Place the oil in a nonstick skillet and put on a stove burner. Set on medium heat.

5. Carefully place the patties in the hot pan, about 1/2-inch apart. You may have to work in batches.

6. Cook one side for 4 minutes, and then flip the cakes over with tongs and fry an additional 4 minutes.

7. Remove the finished crab cakes from the pan.

8. To assemble the sliders, split the slider buns, place a crab cake on the bottom half, followed by a leaf of lettuce. Spread 1 tablespoon of tartar sauce on the top half and place on top of the lettuce. Serve immediately.

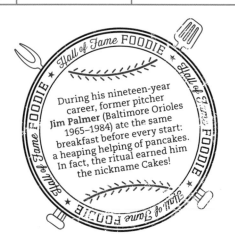

Hall of Fame FOODIE

During his nineteen-year career, former pitcher **Jim Palmer** (Baltimore Orioles 1965–1984) ate the same breakfast before every start: a heaping helping of pancakes. In fact, the ritual earned him the nickname Cakes!

TARTAR SAUCE

PREP	COOK	MAKES
5	**0**	**½**
MINUTES	MINUTES	CUP

	INGREDIENTS	
◇	2	green onions
◇	½ cup	mayonnaise
◇	2 tablespoons	sweet pickle relish
◇	1 teaspoon	Dijon mustard
◇	1 teaspoon	lemon juice
◇	½ teaspoon	salt
◇	¼ teaspoon	ground black pepper
◇		
◇		

1 Chop the green onions finely and add to a mixing bowl.

2 Add remaining ingredients and stir to combine.

3 Serve on Maryland Crab Cake Sliders. Store leftovers in refrigerator for up to 3 days.

BERRY SPRITZER

PREP	COOK	MAKES
5	**0**	**2**
MINUTES	MINUTES	QUARTS

	INGREDIENTS	
◇	1 quart	berry juice
◇	1 quart	sparkling water
◇	handful of each	strawberries
◇		raspberries
◇		blueberries

1 Combine the berry juice and sparkling water in a pitcher. Stir lightly to combine.

2 Pour into glasses with several strawberries, raspberries, and blueberries for garnish.

BOS

Boston Red Sox Baseball Club

FENWAY PARK

LOCATION
Boston, Massachusetts

OPENED
1912

CAPACITY
37,673

NICKNAMES
The Cathedral of Boston

America's Most Beloved Ballpark

Built in 1912, Fenway Park holds the title as the oldest ballpark in Major League Baseball. The stadium was built in an area of Boston called "The Fens," or "Fenway," thus the name. But the park has changed a lot over the years. The Green Monster, a towering 37-foot-tall wall in left field, was added in 1934. The stands are now concrete instead of the original wood. Still, stepping into Fenway Park is like traveling back in baseball history. Greats like Babe Ruth and Ted Williams once called it home. And the Red Sox have won eight World Series titles — starting with one the year Fenway Park opened — in their more than 100-year history.

BOSTON FRANK

with BAKED BEANS

Located on the Atlantic Coast, Boston, Massachusetts is no stranger to seafood, and Fenway fans welcome it with open mouths. From New England eats like lobster rolls and clam chowder to oysters and sushi, the oceanic options can feed a sell-out crowd. But at the league's oldest park, classics are king, and this simple, snappy frankfurter is top dog.

NYY

New York Yankees Baseball Club

YANKEE STADIUM

LOCATION

Bronx, New York

OPENED

2009

CAPACITY

49,642

NICKNAMES

New Yankee Stadium

The House That Steinbrenner Built

The Bronx Bandbox

In 2009, the Yankees moved across the street, literally, from their old stadium to a new ballpark in the Bronx. The name moved with them as it's still called Yankee Stadium. Like the old stadium, the new ballpark has a classic, open feel — the playing field dimensions are even exactly same — only the new Yankee Stadium has some modern amenities like cup holders on all seats, party suites, and a towering, 101-foot wide HD scoreboard. The Bronx Bombers christened the new stadium with their 27th World Series title the year it opened. Oddly enough, they won their first World Series in 1923, when the old Yankee Stadium opened.

STEAK SANDWICH

with CREAMY PEPPERCORN SAUCE & GARLIC POTATO WEDGES

As one of the oldest teams in the league, the Yankees are experienced in providing quality ballpark food, starting with freshly made ribbon fries and famous New York hot dogs. Today, the stadium's food options range widely, from build-your-own-nachos stands to high-end steak joints. But this tender, sky-high steak sandwich will satisfy any Empire State appetite.

STEAK SANDWICH

	INGREDIENTS	
◇	1	medium onion, sliced
◇	1	roasted red pepper
◇	2 tablespoons	olive oil, divided
◇	2 6-ounce	strip steaks
◇	4	ciabatta rolls
◇	dash	salt & pepper
◇	1 ounce	creamy peppercorn sauce
◇		

PREP 10 MINUTES

COOK 25 MINUTES

MAKES 4 SANDWICHES

1 In a skillet, place 1 tablespoon olive oil and heat to medium. Add sliced onion and red pepper. Cook over medium heat until the onions soften and turn slightly brown, stirring occasionally.

2 Meanwhile, on a clean cutting board, season both sides of the steak with salt and pepper.

3 In another skillet, heat the remaining tablespoon of olive oil over medium-high heat.

4 Carefully place the steaks in the pan.

5 Cook for about 6–7 minutes, turn them over with tongs and cook another 6–7 minutes.

6 Remove the steaks, place on a plate, and loosely put foil over them. Allow to sit for 10 minutes.

7 While the steaks rest, prepare rolls by slicing in half crosswise, and make the peppercorn sauce. When the steaks are finished resting, slice thinly.

8 To assemble the sandwiches, spread 2 tablespoons of the peppercorn sauce on the bottom half of each ciabatta roll. Next, add about ¼ of the steak, followed by ¼ of the onion and pepper mix. Top with the second half of the roll. Serve immediately.

SAY WHAT?!

"YOU BETTER CUT THE PIZZA IN FOUR PIECES, BECAUSE I'M NOT HUNGRY ENOUGH TO EAT SIX."

YOGI BERRA
(CATCHER, NEW YORK YANKEES 1946-1963)

CREAMY PEPPERCORN SAUCE

PREP	COOK	MAKES
5	**0**	**4**
MINUTES	MINUTES	OUNCES

INGREDIENTS	
◇ 3 tablespoons	mayonnaise
◇ 3 tablespoons	sour cream
◇ 1 teaspoon	Dijon mustard
◇ ½ teaspoon	Worcestershire sauce
◇ 1 tablespoon	freshly ground pepper
◇ ½ teaspoon	salt

1 Combine all ingredients in a small mixing bowl and stir well.

2 Store any leftovers in an airtight container in the refrigerator for up to 3 days.

GARLIC POTATO WEDGES

PREP	COOK	MAKES
10	**40**	**4**
MINUTES	MINUTES	SERVINGS

INGREDIENTS	
◇ 4	russet potatoes
◇ ¼ cup	olive oil
◇ 2 teaspoons	crushed garlic
◇ 1 teaspoon	salt
◇ ½ teaspoon	ground black pepper
◇ ¼ cup	grated parmesan cheese
◇	

1 Preheat oven to 425°F and line baking sheet with parchment paper. Set aside. Peel and cut the potatoes into wedges.

2 In a mixing bowl, combine the potatoes, olive oil, crushed garlic, salt, and pepper. Stir until the potatoes are well coated.

3 Arrange the potatoes on the baking sheet, about ½ inch apart. Bake in the oven for about 15 minutes and then carefully flip them over using a spatula. Bake for an additional 15 minutes or until golden brown.

4 Sprinkle cheese over the potatoes and return to the oven for another 5–10 minutes or until the cheese is melted and slightly browned.

5 Remove from the oven and allow to cool slightly before serving.

TB

Tampa Bay Rays Baseball Club

TROPICANA FIELD

LOCATION	
St. Petersburg, Florida	
OPENED	
1990	
CAPACITY	
31,042	
NICKNAMES	
The Trop	
The Juicer	

Tropicana Field was a case of "build it, and they will come." The park was completed in 1990, in St. Petersburg, just outside of Tampa, in hopes that a team would eventually call the stadium home. The expansion Tampa Bay Devil Rays joined the American League in 1998. The team's name was later shortened to just "Rays" in 2008. Tropicana Field is unique among modern-day ballparks. It is the only domed baseball stadium still in use, and it is one of just two parks with an artificial playing field. Another feature that sets it apart is its 10,000-gallon Rays Touch Tank, with actual stingrays — not players — just beyond the right-center-field wall.

CUBAN SANDWICH

with FRIED PLANTAINS

Just five hundred miles from Cuba, Tampa, Florida is bursting with Latin influence. In fact, the city was home to the first Cuban community in the United States. So it's no surprise that Tropicana Field is home to tropical drinks and festive foods, including the island's namesake dish: the Cuban. This tangy, meat-stuffed sandwich is always a home run!

CUBAN SANDWICH

PREP
10 MINUTES

COOK
40 MINUTES

MAKES
4 SANDWICHES

INGREDIENTS

◇	1 1-pound	pork tenderloin
◇	generous amount	salt & pepper
◇	2 tablespoons	olive oil
◇	4	ciabatta rolls
◇	4 teaspoons, divided	mustard
◇	12 slices, divided	smoked deli ham
◇	4 slices, divided	Swiss cheese
◇	4	dill pickle spears

YUCKY CHARMS

In 2008, Tropicana Field groundskeepers hung hot dogs inside a stadium locker — a good luck charm to their slumping team. Believe it or not, the Ray's started winning! When the rotting dogs mysteriously disappeared (and the team started losing), a picture of the hot dogs (and a couple of meatballs!) were hung up instead. That year, the Rays competed in the World Series, their most successful season to date.

1 First, prepare the pork. Preheat oven to 375°F. Place tenderloin on a cutting board and season generously with salt and pepper.

2 Place pork tenderloin on a baking sheet and drizzle olive oil over the top.

3 Bake in oven for 30–35 minutes or until no longer pink inside.

4 Remove from oven and cover with foil. Allow to rest for 10 minutes before slicing thinly.

5 To assemble sandwiches, slice each roll crosswise and spread 1 teaspoon of mustard on the bottom half of each.

6 Place 3 slices of ham on top of the mustard.

7 Add about ¼ of the pork slices on top of the ham, followed by a slice of Swiss cheese and a pickle spear.

8 Place the top of the bread on and serve immediately.

FRIED PLANTAINS

PREP	COOK	MAKES
5 MINUTES	5 MINUTES	4 SERVINGS

INGREDIENTS	
◇ 2 large	plantains, ripe
◇ 2 tablespoons	olive oil
◇ 1 teaspoon	salt

1 Peel the plantains and slice into ½-inch rounds.

2 Add oil to a skillet and heat on medium.

3 Carefully add the plantains (Be very careful! There might be splatters!) and cook for about 2 minutes, until golden brown. Flip them over and cook an additional minute.

4 Remove the plantains to a plate lined with paper towels. Sprinkle immediately with salt.

5 Allow to cool for 2 minutes before serving.

THE MUSTARD BULLPEN

While traditional Cuban sandwiches contain yellow mustard, don't be afraid to throw a changeup and sub in one of these mustard varieties:

Spicy Brown   Honey   Whole Grain   Dijon   Hot

TOR

Toronto Blue Jays Baseball Club

ROGERS CENTRE

LOCATION
Toronto, Ontario
OPENED
1989
CAPACITY
49,282
NICKNAMES
SkyDome
The Dome

The Blue Jays are the only Canadian team in the MLB. Their newest ballpark, the Rogers Centre, opened in 1989. It helped begin the era of retractable-roof stadiums, as it was the first ballpark to have one that functioned properly — unlike Olympic Stadium in Montreal, which was the first attempt at a retractable roof. Rogers Centre currently has an artificial playing surface, but team officials and fans alike are hoping a grass field will be installed in the near future. The CFL Argonauts also play at Rogers Centre — the pitcher's mound can be raised or lowered depending on if the home team is playing baseball or football. Also, the Renaissance Hotel is part of the stadium. Visitors can watch games from one of 70 rooms that overlook the playing field.

POUTINE

with APPLE BLONDIES WITH MAPLE GLAZE

Poutine, pronounced poo-TEEN, originated in Quebec, Canada, in the late 1950s. Since then, this hearty dish has become a favorite across the Great White North, including many concession stands at Rogers Centre. A concoction of thick, salty french fries, brown gravy, and cheese curds, this game-day snack is the ultimate triple play.

POUTINE

PREP	COOK	MAKES
15	**35**	**4**
MINUTES	MINUTES	SERVINGS

INGREDIENTS

◇	4	russet potatoes
◇	¼ cup	olive oil
◇	1 ½ teaspoons	salt, divided
◇	1 teaspoon	ground black pepper
◇	2 tablespoons	unsalted butter
◇	2 tablespoons	all-purpose flour
◇	1 ½ cups	beef broth
◇	1 teaspoon	Worcestershire sauce
◇	1 cup	cheddar cheese curds

POUTINE TIME LINE

1957 — Construction worker Eddy Lainesse orders a bag of fries at Café Idéal in Warwick, Quebec, Canada. He asks restaurant owner Fernand Lachance to mix in some cheese curds. The first "poutine" is born.

1964 — The Le Roy Jucep introduces poutine on its menu, complete with brown gravy. Restaurant owner Jean-Paul Roy officially named the concoction "poutine," a Québécois French pronunciation of the word "pudding."

1987 — First major fast food chain adds poutine to its menu.

2014 — "Poutine" is added to the Merriam-Webster dictionary.

2015 — Detroit Tigers unveil poutine hot dog at Comerica Park.

1 Preheat oven to 450°F and line a baking sheet with parchment paper. Set aside.

2 Peel and cut the potatoes into ¼-inch wide sticks, like french fries. Dry well with a paper towel and place in mixing bowl with olive oil, 1 teaspoon salt and ½ teaspoon ground black pepper. Stir until the potatoes are coated.

3 Arrange the potatoes on the baking sheet and place in the oven for 15 minutes, then flipping them with a spatula and baking an additional 15 minutes or until golden brown and crispy.

4 Meanwhile, make the sauce. In a saucepan over medium heat, melt the butter. Add the flour and whisk until the butter has absorbed the flour.

5 While whisking, pour in the broth and add the Worcestershire sauce. Continue to whisk until the sauce begins to bubble. Turn down the heat to a gentle simmer until the sauce thickens, about 5 minutes.

6 Season with ½ teaspoon salt and ½ teaspoon ground black pepper, adding more if necessary.

7 Serve on a large platter with edges, spread the french fries evenly. Sprinkle the cheese all over the fries, and then pour the sauce over the top. Serve immediately.

APPLE BLONDIES WITH MAPLE GLAZE

PREP	COOK	MAKES
15 MINUTES	**35** MINUTES	**12** BLONDIES

	INGREDIENTS	
◇	BLONDIES:	
◇	generous sprays	non-stick cooking spray
◇	½ cup (1 stick)	unsalted butter
◇	2	Granny Smith apples
◇	1 cup	flour
◇	2 teaspoons	ground cinnamon
◇	½ teaspoon	baking powder
◇	¼ teaspoon	baking soda
◇	¼ teaspoon	salt
◇	1	egg
◇	1 cup, packed	dark brown sugar
◇	1 teaspoon	vanilla extract
◇	¼ cup	chopped walnuts
◇		
◇	MAPLE GLAZE:	
◇	½ cup	powdered sugar
◇	¼ cup	pure maple syrup
◇	¼ teaspoon	vanilla extract
◇	2 tablespoons	water or milk
◇		

1. Slowly melt the butter over low heat in a saucepan. Set aside to cool.

2. Preheat oven to 350°F and generously spray a baking dish to prevent sticking.

3. Peel and core the apples, then chop into ½-inch cubes. Set aside.

4. In a large mixing bowl, combine flour, cinnamon, baking powder, baking soda, and salt. Stir to combine.

5. In a second mixing bowl, combine the cooled butter, egg, dark brown sugar, and vanilla extract. Whisk vigorously until the brown sugar is mostly dissolved.

6. Pour the liquids into the flour mixture and stir to combine. Add apples and walnuts, if using. Stir gently and pour into the baking dish.

7. Bake for 35 minutes or until a toothpick comes out clean after piercing the blondie. Allow to cool completely before glazing, about 1 hour.

8. While the blondies are baking, make the glaze. Combine the powdered sugar, maple syrup, vanilla extract, and water or milk in a small mixing bowl. Use a fork to mix until it forms a glaze. Add more water or milk if it is too thick, or more powdered sugar if it is too thin.

9. Finish the blondies by drizzling the glaze over the bars before cutting and serving.

CHW

Chicago White Sox Baseball Club

U.S. CELLULAR FIELD

LOCATION

Chicago, Illinois

OPENED

1991

CAPACITY

40,615

NICKNAMES

The Cell

New Comiskey Park

Opening in 1991 as "new" Comiskey Park — replacing the 81-year-old "old" Comiskey — the home of the White Sox was officially renamed U.S. Cellular Field in 2003. The Cell, as fans call it, towers above the South Side of Chicago, just off the city's busy Dan Ryan Expressway. Fans wandering the concourse can take in sculptures featuring White Sox legends, from Nellie Fox to Paul Konerko. Built just one year before a new wave of retro-style ballparks, many Chicago fans still long for their cozy, fan-friendly stadium of yesteryear. However, continued renovations have increased U.S. Cellular's appeal, and the giant, exploding scoreboard in center field — a holdover from old Comiskey — remains a fan favorite.

CHICAGO-STYLE HOT DOG

with CORN OFF THE COB

Those seeking the South Side's finest fare have a wealth of options. Dining staples include the city's famous deep-dish pizza and this Chicago-style hot dog, loaded with onions, relish, and a pickle spear. Fans also line up to chow down on the Cell's famous corn off the cob — sweet corn loaded with cheese and soaked in everything from butter to mayonnaise!

CLE

Cleveland Indians Baseball Club

PROGRESSIVE FIELD

LOCATION
Cleveland, Ohio
OPENED
1994
CAPACITY
38,000
NICKNAME
The Jake

The Indians opened their 1994 season playing in Jacobs Field. But The Jake's naming rights were later purchased, and the park is now called Progressive Field. Before the move to their new stadium, the team was considered one of the worst clubs in baseball. Shortly afterward, they made two trips to the World Series, only to lose both times, and were selling out games left and right. When the stadium's massive scoreboard was installed in 2004, it was the largest in all of sports. Recent renovations at Progressive Field have expanded the view of downtown Cleveland as well as added restaurants, social spaces, and other modern amenities.

PARMESAN-GARLIC POPCORN

with NUTTY CHOCOLATE DRIZZLE POPCORN & WATERMELON LEMONADE

Indians fans can go from downtown Cleveland to Progressive Field through the center-field entrance, which means there's a plethora of food choices in the area. But one of the stadium's signature foods is as classic as baseball itself: popcorn! This crunchy hand-snack is sold in several varieties throughout the park. Salty or sweet, popcorn is always a treat.

PARMESAN-GARLIC POPCORN

PREP	COOK	MAKES
5	5	6
MINUTES	MINUTES	SERVINGS

	INGREDIENTS	
◇	2 ounces	parmesan cheese
◇	3 tablespoons	butter
◇	1 cup	popping corn
◇	1 tablespoon	oil
◇	2 teaspoons	garlic salt
◇		

1 Shred the cheese using the small holes of a box grater, then melt the butter over low heat in a small saucepan. Set aside.

2 Add the oil and popping corn to the large pot and cover with lid. Set over medium heat until you start to hear the corn popping. Slide the pot back and forth over the heating element until you no longer hear the kernels popping. Remove from heat immediately.

3 Carefully pour the popped corn into a large mixing bowl and add the butter, cheese, and garlic salt. Mix well. Serve immediately.

WATERMELON LEMONADE

PREP	COOK	MAKES
10	0	2
MINUTES	MINUTES	QUARTS

	INGREDIENTS	
◇	4 cups	watermelon, chopped
◇	6 cups	lemonade
◇		

1 Place watermelon in a blender. Blend until pureed.

2 Place a sieve over the pitcher and pour watermelon puree through it. Discard the pulp left over.

3 Pour lemonade into the pitcher. Stir to combine. Pour in glasses with ice cubes.

NUTTY CHOCOLATE DRIZZLE POPCORN

PREP	COOK	MAKES
10 MINUTES	5 MINUTES	6 SERVINGS

	INGREDIENTS	
◇	1 cup	popping corn
◇	3 tablespoons	oil
◇	½ cup	semisweet chocolate chips
◇	½ cup	peanut butter chips
◇	¼ cup	butter
◇	½ cup	powdered sugar
◇		

1 Add the oil and popping corn to the large pot and cover with lid. Set over medium heat until you start to hear the corn popping. Slide the pot back and forth over the heating element until you no longer hear the kernels popping. Remove from heat immediately and set aside.

2 In a microwave-safe bowl, add the semisweet chocolate chips, peanut butter chips, and butter. Microwave at 50% for 30 seconds, then stir. Microwave an additional 30 seconds or until the chips and butter are melted and smooth.

3 Place the popped corn in a mixing bowl and drizzle the chocolate mixture over. Stir until all the popcorn is coated.

4 Sprinkle powdered sugar on top and mix until coated. Allow to rest for at least 30 minutes before serving.

POP ICON

Looking for an alternative to cooking popcorn with oil? Try an air popper, which pops corn kernels with hot air. In the mid-1970s, one of the first air poppers was invented in Cleveland, Ohio, making the city a true pop icon!

Detroit Tigers Baseball Club

COMERICA PARK

LOCATION
Detroit, Michigan
OPENED
2000
CAPACITY
41,574
NICKNAMES
Comerica National Park
CoPa

Tigers don't roam just the outfield in downtown Detroit's Comerica Park. From the fifteen-foot tiger statue at the entrance to the two perched atop the left-field scoreboard — whose eyes light up after Detroit home runs and victories — the big cats are everywhere. Fans more interested in the baseball variety of Tigers enjoy Comerica Park's throwback-style field, complete with a strip of dirt between home plate and the pitcher's mound, as well as the Detroit skyline, visible over the left-field fence. Kids and adults alike delight in the park's fifty-foot Ferris wheel, complete with a dozen baseball-shaped cars that can seat up to five passengers each.

CONEY DOG

with ONION RINGS & APPLE CHERRY PUNCH

Comerica Park, built in 2000, caters to baseball fans who prefer more standard ballpark fare. Stadium favorites include street tacos, onion rings, and good old-fashioned corn dogs. But Coney Dogs fuel Detroit Tigers fans. Serve these meat-sauce-topped dogs with a side of thick onion rings and a sweet, refreshing punch for the ultimate Motor City meal.

KC

Kansas City Royals Baseball Club

KAUFFMAN STADIUM

LOCATION
Kansas City, Missouri
OPENED
1973
CAPACITY
37,903
NICKNAMES
The K

Formerly known as Royals Stadium, Kauffman Stadium strikes the perfect blend between historic and modern amenities. It's the sixth-oldest big-league stadium still in use, yet its progressive architecture and an extensive 2009 remodel keep it feeling modern and new. The ballpark's trademark feature is its 322-foot waterfall display in center field, complete with fountains that spray water into the air before the game and between innings. Fans with a taste for baseball history can visit statues of Royals greats George Brett, Dick Howser, and Frank White in right field.

BARBECUE RIBS

with PICKLES

Kansas City proclaims itself the barbecue capital of America, and Kauffman Stadium doesn't fail to live up to that title. Fans can enjoy a rack of barbecued ribs, either on the concourse or in the countless rib joints sprinkled all around town. Pair that with some home-style pickles for a true Kansas City dining experience.

MIN

Minnesota Twins Baseball Club

TARGET FIELD

LOCATION
Minneapolis, Minnesota
OPENED
2010
CAPACITY
39,021

After decades of playing inside the cavernous Metrodome, the Minnesota Twins stepped back out under the sky with the opening of Target Field in 2010. The new ballpark provides spectacular views of downtown Minneapolis along with being a great venue for baseball. The stadium's relatively small footprint gives it a cozy, intimate feeling, while its downtown location has revitalized the city. The park's most distinct feature, a giant mechanical sign of the Twins's original team logo, illuminates in center field during home run celebrations.

CHEDDAR-BACON STUFFED BURGER

with APPLE PIE-ON-A-STICK

Fans needn't go home hungry at Target Field! Food options throughout the stadium feature local faves, including walleye, wild rice soup, and just about anything on a stick — a Minnesota State Fair tradition. Those looking for the Twin Cities' most famous dish can head to the upper concourse for a "Jucy Lucy," a hamburger stuffed with molten cheese.

SAFECO FIELD

LOCATION
Seattle, Washington
OPENED
1999
CAPACITY
47,574
NICKNAMES
The Safe

Located in downtown Seattle, Safeco Field offers fans the best of both worlds. A retractable roof allows fans to see the Seattle skyline and Puget Sound sunsets on clear evenings, while keeping the field dry during the Pacific Northwest's frequent rain showers. "The Safe" is a classic baseball park, with real grass and flawless sight lines. The park's famous chandelier, constructed of 1,000 resin baseball bats, hangs over the home plate entrance, while "the Mitt" is a 9-foot bronze baseball glove and popular photo opportunity.

SANDWICH SUSHI

with SWEET SUSHI

Safeco mirrors Seattle in its wide range of food choices, from fresh sushi to barbecue to spicy pad thai. Fans in the mood for something a bit heavier can enjoy the stadium's garlic fries and bacon-wrapped hot dogs. After the game, fans have a wealth of choices in nearby restaurants, from Korean steakhouses to oyster joints to traditional sports grills.

TEX

GLOBE LIFE PARK
IN ARLINGTON

LOCATION
Arlington, Texas
OPENED
1994
CAPACITY
48,114
NICKNAMES
The Ballpark in Arlington
The Temple
The Globe

Completed in 1994, the Rangers' ballpark has gone through several name changes before settling on Globe Life Park. The park was built at a time when many other stadiums were drawing on past ballparks for inspiration, thus Globe Life Park's red-brick facade and arches. There is even a brick Walk of Fame inside the park that displays information of past Rangers. And some legends of the game, from strikeout king Nolan Ryan to phenom catcher Ivan Rodriquez have donned Rangers uniforms.

STEAK FAJITAS

with PECAN PIE BITES

The state of Texas is known for doing things big, and that carries over to its ballpark food. The stadium doesn't just offer foot-long dogs as the Choomongous is a two-foot-long beef teriyaki sandwich topped with spicy slaw. And then there's bacon — from bacon cotton candy to bacon-wrapped hot dogs and bacon on a stick.

STEAK FAJITAS

	PREP	COOK	MAKES
	10 MINUTES	**15** MINUTES	**4** FAJITAS

	INGREDIENTS	
◇	2 6-ounce	strip steaks
◇	1	bell pepper
◇	1	medium onion
◇	1 tablespoon	olive oil
◇	1 teaspoon	salt
◇	½ teaspoon	ground black pepper
◇	1 teaspoon	cumin
◇	1 teaspoon	chili powder
◇	¼ teaspoon	cayenne pepper
◇	8	flour tortillas
◇ ◇	optional toppings: grated cheese, sour cream, and guacamole (see page 65)	

1 Slice the steaks thinly and set aside.

2 Cut the top off the pepper, and then slice in half lengthwise. Scoop out the seeds and white parts. Slice into ¼-inch strips and set aside.

3 Peel and slice the onion into ¼-inch strips and set aside.

4 In a skillet, heat the oil over medium-high heat. When the oil is hot, add the steak. Cook for about 5 minutes, stirring every minute or two. After the meat has browned, reduce the heat to medium and then add the peppers, onions, salt, pepper, cumin, chili powder, and cayenne pepper.

5 Sauté for an additional 10 minutes or until the vegetables have begun to soften.

6 To assemble, place some meat/onion/pepper mixture into flour tortillas along with desired toppings and serve immediately.

TOP DOG

Where can you find the Major League's largest hot dog? Texas, of course! At Globe Life Park, hungry fans can take a crack at the "Boomstick," a two-foot-long hot dog covered in chili, cheese, and onions. The record-breaking (and gut-busting) dog is named after former Ranger right fielder Nelson Cruz's moniker (Texas Rangers, 2006–2013).

PECAN PIE BITES

PREP	COOK	MAKES
10 MINUTES	2 HOURS	16 BITES

	INGREDIENTS	
◇	12	pecan shortbread cookies
◇	4 ounces	cream cheese,
◇		softened to
◇		room temperature
◇	1/4 teaspoon	vanilla extract
◇	3/4 pound	vanilla almond bark
◇	1/4 cup	pecan chips

1 In a zip-top bag, put the cookies in and seal closed. Smash with a rolling pin until crushed into small crumbs.

2 Add the crumbs to a mixing bowl along with the cream cheese and vanilla extract. Stir until combined and then scoop out even tablespoons and roll between hands to make balls.

3 Set on a cookie sheet and refrigerate for 1 hour to set.

4 Meanwhile, melt the vanilla almond bark in a saucepan over low heat, stirring occasionally, and line a baking sheet with parchment paper and set aside.

5 When the bites are finished setting, drop one in the almond bark and remove with two forks, allowing the excess to drip off.

6 Carefully place on the lined baking sheet and sprinkle it with a pinch of pecan chips. Repeat for the rest of the bites.

7 Place dipped bites in refrigerator for an additional hour to set the coating before serving. Store in airtight container in refrigerator for up to 3 days.

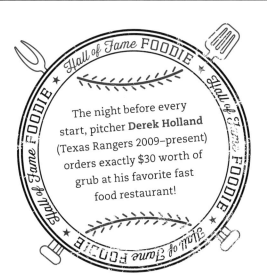

Hall of Fame FOODIE

The night before every start, pitcher **Derek Holland** (Texas Rangers 2009–present) orders exactly $30 worth of grub at his favorite fast food restaurant!

About the Author

Katrina Jorgensen is a graduate of
Le Cordon Bleu College of Culinary Arts.
She enjoys creating new recipes and sharing
them with friends and family. She lives in
Rochester, Minnesota, with her husband,
Tony, and dog, Max.

Ballpark Cookbook The American League is published by
Capstone Press
1710 Roe Crest Drive, North Mankato, Minnesota 56003
www.mycapstone.com

Sports Illustrated KIDS is a trademark of Time Inc. Used with permission.

Cataloging-in-Publication Data is available on the Library of Congress website.
ISBN: 978-1-4914-8232-2 (library hardcover)
ISBN: 978-1-4914-8622-1 (eBook PDF)

Contributing Writers: Blake A. Hoena and Donald Lemke
Editor: Donald Lemke
Designer: Bob Lentz
Art Director: Heather Kindseth
Media Researcher: Eric Gohl
Food Stylist: Sarah Schuette
Production Specialist: Tori Abraham

Photo Credits:
Newscom: Icon Sportswire DCK/Dan Hamilton, 20, Robert Harding/Aaron Mccoy, 56; Shutterstock: Alhovik, 47 (pizza box),
andersphoto, 31 (bottom popcorn), Brent Hofacker, cover (hot dog), Eric Broder Van Dyke, 52, Ffooter, 24, 40, Heath Oldham, 4, Joe
Belanger, 34 (bottom chili dogs), Julia Ivantsova, 1 (pencil), 64 (pencil), Margie Hurwich, cover (stadium), Mark Ross, 43 (baseballs),
Moises Fernandez Acosta, cover (mustard bottle), 19 (mustard bottles), Odua Images, 42 (cereal box), Richard Cavalleri, 12, Seregam,
62–63 (tape measure), Stuart Monk, 1 (chili dog); Sports Illustrated: Bob Rosato, 16, Damian Strohmeyer, 8, 28, David E. Klutho, 36,
60, John Biever, 32, 44, Robert Beck, 48

All recipe photographs by Capstone Studio: Karon Dubke.

All other images and design elements provided by Shutterstock.

Printed in Canada.
092015   009223FRS16